x

a blewointment book

NIGHTWOOD EDITIONS

2013

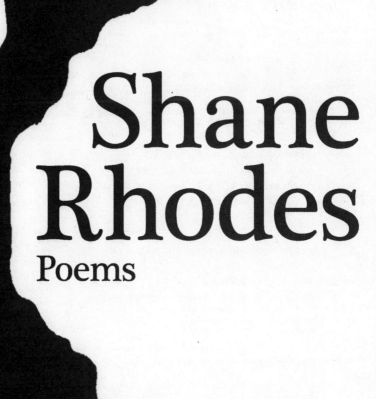

Shane
Rhodes

Poems

Nightwood Editions
P.O. Box 1779
Gibsons, BC V0N 1V0
Canada
www.nightwoodeditions.com

Nightwood Editions acknowledges financial support from the Government of Canada through the Canada Book Fund and the Canada Council for the Arts, and from the Province of British Columbia through the British Columbia Arts Council and the Book Publisher's Tax Credit.

This book has been produced on 100% post-consumer recycled, ancient-forest-free paper, processed chlorine-free and printed with vegetable-based dyes.

Cover design: Carleton Wilson
Interior design: Shane Rhodes

Printed and bound in Canada

Library and Archives Canada Cataloguing in Publication

Rhodes, Shane, 1973-, author
    X / Shane Rhodes.

"A blewointment book".
Poems.
ISBN 978-0-88971-288-1 (pbk.)

    I. Title.

PS8585.H568X12 2013   C811'.6   C2013-903105-7

Contents

You Are Here 8

Preoccupied Space 10

Found Land. 28

Acts. 63

Notes & Acknowledgements 80

White Noise 89

You Are Here

Though not endorsed by the treaty commissioner, I would like to
acknowledge this book was written in the said country
While this book was written, contested territory was tested
I would like to acknowledge the Secwepemc, the Cree and the
Algonquin nations, upon whose territories this book was written
The land was "shovel ready"
I would like to acknowledge I did not ask for permission, that
I felt too uncomfortable to ask and didn't know how to, that
I don't know if asking is the answer because I barely know the
questions
I would, however, like my acknowledgement to be acknowledged
Warning: this book is not about distant lands, Greek and Roman
philosophers, Japanese haiku masters, and Elizabethan poets will
not be discussed
This book is about desire
the desire to look elsewhere
This book is about where I live, a place still settling, still making
the land—law by law, arrest by arrest, jail by jail—its own
snow blown
As stipulated in subparagraph 12(1)(a)(iv), paragraph 12(1)(b)
or sub-section 12(2) or under subparagraph 12(1)(a)(iii) pursu-
ant to an order made under subsection 109(2), a dispute cannot
be made under this section of my book
Warning: this book of verse demands more of verse, this book
demands perversity
This book uses words as heard in annual reports and business pro-
spectus, the smooth cadence of policy platforms and parliament-
ary committees, the shouts of protesters and riot police
This book, also known as *The Heart of Whiteness*, terries in In-
dian Territory, my terra firma, where all intercourse is, of course,
governed by the official *Indian Intercourse Act*

Making land: here is a YouTube loop of me stepping from my Legend twelve-foot Ultralite aluminum boat with its Mercury 2.5-HP four-stroke engine, book in hand, claiming all this as my new found land

This book, also entitled *What??*, is part of my much larger Amnesia Project, created with generous support from the Ministry for Elective Memory

This book is new—groundbreaking   people moving   tree clearing   root pulling   concrete pouring   factory building   new

Tired of maintaining the holes in its language, tired of staying silent, so tired of forgetting, this book

This book, marking its territory on virgin snow and barking at the fenceline, is about the settlers' dream of legitimacy

Warning: the reading of this book while at a game between the Eskimos, Blackhawks, Braves or Indians, sponsored by Mohawk Gas, within a vat of melted Land o Lakes sweet cream salted butter, chewing Red Man tobacco, while listening to "Indian Giver" by the Ramones, may be dangerous to your health

This book was written in the gaps between words written and words spoken, words meant and words meant only to fill the space of meaning

This book I will continue to write until I get it right, and I will never get it right

About a land held by therefores, herebys and hereinafters, this book

    la terre de ma mère

This terrible book, with its interracial terroir, was written on an interrogated territory of error

This book was written on land shipped to China, manufactured into products free of history, and sold back to us free of thought

Warning: reading this book could be harmful. See this picture of Jim, he has cancer and says, "I wish I'd never started reading"

PREOCCUPIED SPACE

They arrived aboard a sturdy new Model A Ford which had carried them from
I sailed from Norwich on the S.S. *Canada* in He left England and arrive
Jimmy Wong left his family in China was born in Plymouth, Engla
Cuthbert and came to Canada.
Walter came from Poland via France nada.

from Reading

(address gone

She came

"from Doucester Street"

(pronunciation suspect

from factory jobs

(locations unknown

Bob and I were both borne in England and came to

Derwedymouth Navy on

came from Aberdeen

I came

England to B

Went

She left England Sardinia in 1885

He went out to join his brother.

and surely from Toronto

was educated and grew up.

Born in Sussex, he

After to his emigrated from Ire-

Ab came from Iowa

Winnifred and her mother emigrated from Ire-

from a boat crossing

(details lost

in a grandaughter's

closet

from London

lost

"three days in fog and ice pack"
and seventy-foot waves

["Oh, god, give me my corset.
I think I'm going to die."

the boat purling its screws
through the north Atlantic

from a sea of particulars

the fragmented facts

(she would never touch the sea again)

out of the pounding coiling recoiling

pistons driving twin propeller shafts

[250 revolutions per ton of Yorkshire coal]

pushed into the present by burning the past

after three months of ships and trains
threading the Atlantic
and North American Plate

It all began in Argyllshire where I became a sea captain

In 1934, they sold the farm and returned to England

After leaving Oxford, he went out to Assam to manage a

and to raise poultry on the Isle of

I came from

second class steamer

The entire family of Germany came from England

Born in Germany

Stanley was barely 16 when her father bought a

at 15 he left home and after reading the novel

Horace, known as   emigrated to Canada from county Wicklow

Bay

we found ourselves

here

seventy-five miles from Grease Creek

12

from the few words of women
recorded
in my grandmother's journal
barely started
(what time did she have
after cooking twenty years for priests
then losing her mind in dementia
half complete
yellow at the edges
(stored in my mother's filing cabinet
under "Other"

tation then his father offered to pay is way to Canada   I hauled coal from Sheerness M
They returned in '53 and left for the west coast and St. Michael's   they came from Nebra   Michael's Indian School at Alert
"...ia" emigrated with his wife and family from famine from England to work on Dartmoor
"...on the Megantic, a 14,900   her uncle on the old Vancouver steam liner
in July 1896, she sailed with

on page thirty
after a period
and three hard returns

my grandmother
wound the ribbon
around the spool
and would never touch
her typewriter again

(there is a pattern

from the first house

the one before
the one I never knew

handsawn poplar and spruce

"you could see stars
through the ceiling cracks"

later   they rented a shack

owned   by "a bronc rider"

("Boney Thompson

part white   part Indian"

the newness

"a beautiful man"

must have stunned
her

for sixty years

my grandmother

collected books
about the Queen

and, every night,

rowed herself

back across

the North Atlantic

Why do I write this story now, my mother dead [said grandmother] six years ago... Hard times plagued us, and m... detrained and travelled over the virgin prairie in a wagon... emigrated from... city of Tver in Esthon... (oo peop...)... Clarence and his family came up fro... In the spring of 1905,... His father, mother, and their seven children emigrated from... I was born in New York City,

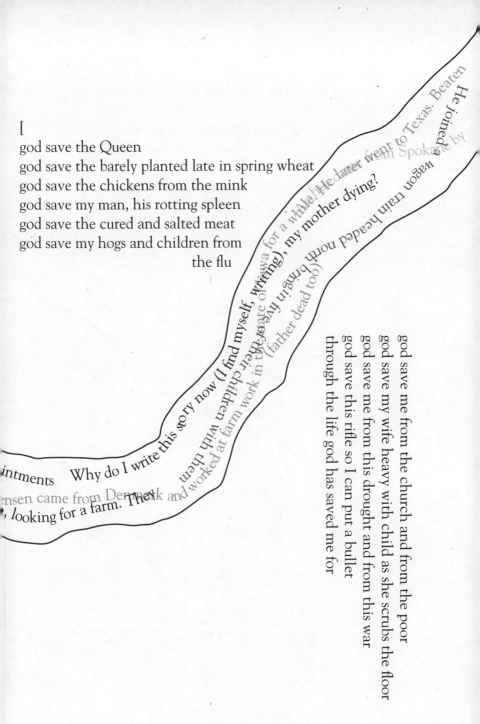

[
god save the Queen
god save the barely planted late in spring wheat
god save the chickens from the mink
god save my man, his rotting spleen
god save the cured and salted meat
god save my hogs and children from
                    the flu

god save me from the church and from the poor
god save my wife heavy with child as she scrubs the floor
god save me from this drought and from this war
god save this rifle so I can put a bullet
through the life god has saved me for

Why do I write this story now (I find myself, writing), nwa for a while. He later went to Texas. Beaten the estate of their children with them and worked at farm work in (father dead too) my mother dying? bringin livestock (over their children dead too) om Spokane by He joined by wagon train headed north

intments
ensen came from Denmark and, looking for a farm. They

these women
　　　　　　　stone faced stone backed stone hands
these are my sources
　　　　　　lost　　through marriage
　　　　　　　　　they had so little need for men
　　　　who got them with child
　　　　　　　and parted from work and drink
　　　　　　　　　only by death
each woman　　unto herself
　　　　　　　　a country

my other grandmother
　　　　　　　　her story
arriving sometime　 (no one
　　　knows when
　　　　　　　last century
she moved
　　　to cheap land

When French had his toes frozen he got an Indian Medicine Man t
her Scandi... Bound for Canada, driving a tea
Billy left Randolf, Iowa ... ancestors, I knew I had
You just dro... she nev...

In the summer of 1893, Billy and his ... came and you were near a house you didn't ...

In those days, when night came and you were ... Dorothy's house ...
Eddie ... came out from China so ... Emer was asked to take ... the first tra ... After the railway was b...

she moved
to Fargo
"the house
set afire
with cattail torches
in Lakota raids"

she moved
(the documents show
to Stone County

wâwâskêsiw-sîpihk

the horses sick
with swamp fever

the river

it moved her

("she" meaning great-
greatgrandmother as
this is the story I give
my grandmother that
her mother should
have told her

ho put Puffball on French's feet. French lost his toes but did not get gangrene.
s and a covered wagon. I kissed horses, and you knew in a barrel.
t sound before when I was coming under in harvest you were welcome. Supe-
w down the lines, unharnessed after had to be carried rth shores of Lac come.
d to take time off to run a

           they built a log cabin on the overland route
                 no rail   rich earth
   stone coal timber
               above the Red Deer

      was said
                          many stopped for a good mîcisowin
says 1974 *Pioneers and Progress*
      binding broke

                                  "even an Indian
                          [nêhiyaw? siksiká?

      duct-taped spine
            pages torn and missing
   till the duct tape broke

                               and a Negro
                     who slept in Pa's chair"

        night's rest

From so much crossing and recrossing of seas,

I always come back

to land

up from Haynes Creek

(no, not Grease Creek

this grandmother   so easy with

words

never kept a journal

Joseph Todd and his family travelled from Michigan in 1913 from Denmark *prairie schooner. The Charlie l* *"Modern-day visitors must feel much like early western settlers who were* *Adam Christiansenn and family arrived in* *is someone to guide you when* *On the day we were leaving Oregon,*

treaty 6 land

wâwâskêsiw-sîpiy

the first house

falling apart

(the chinks stuffed

with moss and manure

the quarter section

cleared

of trees and stone

by hand

of deer and moose

by a .30-06

of people

by words

[before it's forgotten: the homestead   I don't know if it's
still there   my father sold the land   five years ago   last time
I saw it   the walls   collapsed   (when it was abandoned,
he drove a car through   the back wall   I don' t know why   I
struggled through   the thistle   to feel the   pulse in the door
barely there   roughcut lumber   planed from logs   pulled from
the river in spring breakup   insulation of woodchips mouseshit
and three layers of sweaters   that didn't come off until spring
handpump in a shed across   the weedchoked yard   it creaked in
my hand   the leathers cracked   wood stove by the door   long
gone   that stove must have burned red with hand-split poplar
        chunks of coal from the river strip mine   as a kid I remember
                this place   already derelict   curtains strewn across
                        broken glass   cutlery in the drawer   one day,
                        someone had had enough   of history   and
                        left   for the city   but they could never
                                tear it down   this place so full of
                                someone else's memories don't
                                        wander too far   though
She   the floor full   of
a n d   wood
her hus-   rot
band   worked
as hired hands—
she in the kitchen he
in the fields—and cleared this
land   piling rocks   pulling roots
their bodies   shaped by work and chores
that word   so close to song

lls, Montana
Abitibi Consol
worked on the Railroad
then more red-uniformed, horse-riding Mountie
in a car accident. We had six children at the time. In the Spring of 1951, we
the fall of 1902. He liked nothing
He drove a team and wagon to Canada. He filed on a hom
nice to know that there
timber

19

Larkin land
      Stone land
the holes for the witness posts
    pounded down
        through the survey
           land registry
two feet six inches of dirt and clay
(you can still hear the pounding

      [by Charles Magrath, DLS, DTS, in 1892
      or maybe Angus McFee or AE Fardcomb?

stitching the grand trunk through

for this   all these men   played
                  cowboys and Indians
     with themselves

signed treaties
      with themselves

for land surveyed
    by themselves

recorded
    on their own paper
        with their own words
           in their own ink

I once thought
fence posts
with their barbed
wire script
wrote the first stories

but I was wrong
and missed the words
behind the fences
the ones I never learned
and no one ever told me

the stories that say
what I'm living in

this

isn't history

has been drawn to a modification
a pig, and drive it off into the bush
and hence derive the
brother. In 19
homesteaded by J.E. Morgan in 1901. My parents came to Canada in

I WENT WEST WITH MY and Compass EARLY IN APRIL, 1917. WE ARRIVED IN POU

to Canada in that distance to the pig and

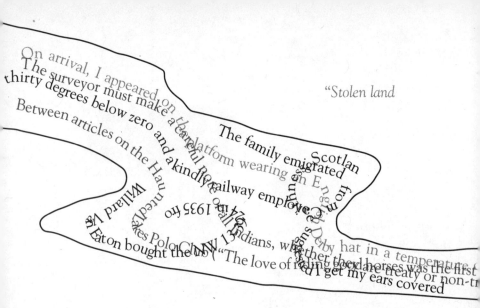

"Stolen land

—those are"

        says the white archivist
        handing me the document

        "loaded words not supported by the

kayâs âcimowin kâ-masinahamihk."

"The Dominion Township Grid system is the cheapest method of producing the most surveyed acres in the shortest time. However, it has been proven to have had a marked effect on the cultural and psychological development of the settlers."

from reading
to gaze   through journals   computer screens
  to ask history with its bloodshot eyes   smudged
with correction fluid   and printer's ink

The archivist brings out the books   and microfilm
she is a keeper   of this place   this museum
of written things   where the plumbing drips
the pipes   burst   with each cold snap
          (a brigade of volunteers   whose only job
                    to rescue the books from leaks

[curved text following the river shape:]

y people were of English descent two or three generations — those old warriors where he met — ny an early pioneer") and the United Farm Women of Alberta in 1897 — ns, found in occupation of lands at the time of subdivision — which we have held from time immemorial, often — Wing Wong was born in Canton, China — came to Canada — Sitting Bull from pioneers who settled — White Cloud — At the age of — murdered in their names went to war — of blood, are — the Dakotas — Montana — years ago — in the winter of — a desperado named C.B. — the quarter sections they occupy, are — "Indian schooners" — please look at the picture "Indians, Frank!"

So much to remember   to hold
in place   every story   with its
serial number incomplete   unpublished
unheard   broken off mid   telling
the pen leaked the journal   dropped
in water the speaker's   mouth
filled with small   pox
their voices   barely
rise off   the page

I listen to the
archivist's gurney
ferrying books
from dark rooms
          to this side
                    of history

sôniyâwahkêsîs

on highway 12   how many years ago   that night
a dark so clear   I could see   the northern lights

it must have been a party   I was driving home
alone   too much to drink
the windshield   hammered   with starspark
                              fox   blur
                                                              of white

        I don't know   why you were there
                        at the roadside   howling
            at the roiling sky
                              that night

In the fall of 1945, the SE 3-39-24 and the West half of NE 3 was bought
Our friends the whites they have been taking our lands away from us and the
ExxonMobil / 275,891 Kg / waterborne ethylene glycol
Born in Holland, he came in 1927   John came to Canada in 1907 from

                        you made no sound as I hit you
only the shock   as two bodies   fox and machine
                        merged   in motion

        I stopped a mile on
                my head against the steering wheel
                    got out and picked your fur   from the chrome
        wiped your blood splatter   from the hood
    and stood   in the cold   the dance above
                            shivered   a little brighter

                        I drove home
        washed my hands

                    fell asleep

Caledonia   London   Paris (pop 11,177)
Nova _____   New _____   New _____   New _____
                        dream names
from dream people
                    (like my grandmothers) off boats and planes
backs stooped   (like my mothers)
from the weight of the continents they carry

        listen to them   pounding their nations down
                into this dream land
        church spires   schools   land registries
(grandmother and her shack
                    you can still hear the pounding
                each pointed roof crescent and cross
                    another nail in the fortress

LA by Julius and Alice who have resided ... my people forever. This land
This you can have. who ... This is for me ... to the present day. This land
nothing left to ... out 10 ... and everything that we use they stop us from using it
SA and then spent ... and everything that we use they stop us
Born in Wiltshire, my mother and I emigrated in August

        with a breath
            full of diesel   and disease
                we took the land
        with a hand full of seeds   and land deeds

the cemeteries are full of them
            the occupiers   the conquerors
        the ones so different from us
                    you can read their journals
            stare at their black and white photographs
their gravestones   covered in birdshit   and moss
            lined with English prayer
                    in Roman font

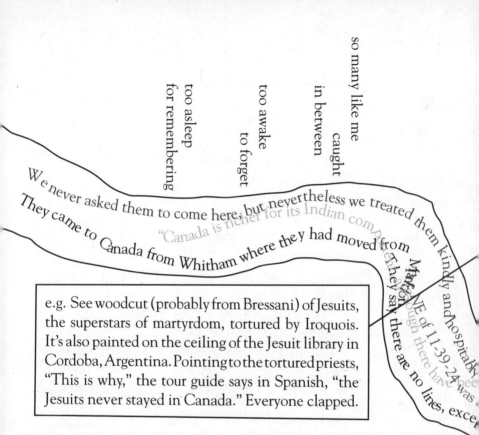

so many like me
in between
caught

too awake
to forget

too asleep
for remembering

We never asked them to come here, but nevertheless we treated them kindly and hospitably

They came to Canada from Whitham where they had moved from

"Canada is richer for its Indian component"

Make NE of 11-39-24...

they say there are no lines, excep...

although there have been was...

e.g. See woodcut (probably from Bressani) of Jesuits, the superstars of martyrdom, tortured by Iroquois. It's also painted on the ceiling of the Jesuit library in Cordoba, Argentina. Pointing to the tortured priests, "This is why," the tour guide says in Spanish, "the Jesuits never stayed in Canada." Everyone clapped.

sôniyâwahkêsîs,
for twenty years   you were nothing
until I saw you this spring

at the unthreaded seam
between   sleep   and waking

that same white fur
howling   now

at the traffic lights   on Preston Street
barking down   the satellites
and high-voltage power lines
that cut through every moment of your sleep

sôniyâwahkêsîs,
you are history   I think
but not the one I was taught

you live now
at the back of my brain
that cage of thought
howling
if I live in this place
if I live in this time
live in it   fully
not in a copy of Europe

not in a present
with no memory
not in the immigrant mind
the children
of settlers carry
that nation
is a dream
nation
held
in the clouds
by drill stems
mine shafts
and plows

that nation   lives in towers
of steel and glass
slaughters   forgets
and never gets dirty
learn   you growl
learn and listen
or close your eyes
and go back to sleep

n diversity could.
them all we
bought by CE Mills, who
make. They have taken possession of all the Indian country and claim it as their own.

Born and raised in the German Village of Sels, Russia, immigra
of little value to many Canad
I came over it owing to the depression. In 1939, I came from
later dropped the Queen M
From Poland, I am at 25   *Ralph a*

FOUND LAND

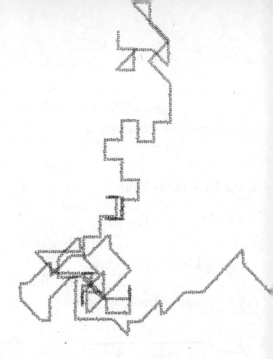

"following its sinuosities

whatever their course may be"

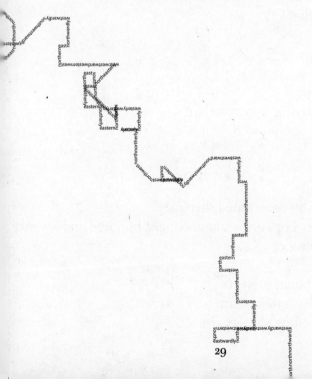

the place of commencement

beginning
from the mouth
our starting point
at the Blackfoot Crossing of the Bow River
at Manitoba Post
in this present year 1899
I started
this fifteenth day of September
respectively
finally
we anchored off the mouth
where the North river flows out of the main stream
where no white man would have any claims
we found the Indians
we found many
we conferred
we drifted
we had grave doubts
we were then carrying a great weight
we came to the conclusion
we treated
we had to
and we left
on the several dates mentioned therein
in the year of Our Lord one thousand eight hundred and seventy
on this day of October
commencing
to preserve her Indian subjects
to deliberate upon certain matters of interest
to Her Most Gracious Majesty

of the one part
and the said Indians
of the other
each performed their several duties
to our great satisfaction
beginning
at a point where the "Suicide"
made and concluded
begins
WE, the undersigned
Indians of Wapiscow
Fairford
Athabasca
we and our children
we thank thee
we thank thee
we thank you (commissioners)
from our hearts
we pray
that we may be saved
from the evil
within
from Fort Garry westward
from Her Majesty
begin again
Indians of the said
Indians of the other
so long as the fur bearing animals remain
in the year of Our Lord
we begin again
on this day of
commencing
at the place of
beginning

the promises herein contained
treaty one

          the said made
       country   and concluded
  the said   notified
Indians   and informed
the said   defined
  Indians   and described
    the said   bounded
      tract   and described
       that is   described
        to say   and defined
          as   know
      aforesaid and be assured
       the said   chosen
   Commissioner   and named
  the purposes   to have
   aforesaid   and to hold
   the said   year
   district   by year
    the said   bounty
   Lieutenant   and benevolence
    the purpose to conduct
     aforesaid and sign
    the said   themselves
   Indians   and their people
    that is   bind
    to say   and pledge
    the said   cede, release
     line   surrender
        and   yield

body of text
treaty one

from the mouth
thence northward to the centre of White Mouth
Lake   issuing therefrom to the mouth
thereof in Winnipeg   to its mouth
in the mouth
of Drunken River   and the mouth
of Swan Creek   set the hand
(Broken Finger)

that tract of country
treaty two

so much land

so much land

near which a fallen elm tree now lies

so much land

north of the creek

so much land

Poplar & Spruce

"Willows, grass"

good sized timber

Good 'Tie' timber

They promise
and engage
that they will
obey
and abide
by the law,
that they will
maintain
peace
good order
between
each other,
themselves
other tribes
between
themselves
Her Majesty's
subjects,
Indians
or
whites,
inhabiting
or hereafter
to inhabit
any part
of the
said
ceded

two hoes
one spade
one plough
five har
rows one
scythe one
axe one
cross-cut
saw one
handsaw
one pit
saw files
grindstone
one aug
er one
chest of
ordin
ary
tools wheat
barley
potatoes
oats the
yoke

and
land
broken

Reeds, mud Bank

36

prepositions
treaty four

to negotiate a treaty
to deliberate
to open up for settlement
to Her Majesty
to obtain the consent
to the Indians
to count upon
to name
to be taken
to be founded
to be made
to become responsible
to the said
to the lands
to the mouth
to its source
to a point
to have
to hold
to diminish
to break up the land
to inhabit

forever
for ever
for all
for every
for ourselves
for each
for settlement, mining
for public works or building
for the purpose of making Treaties
therefore
for Her Majesty the Queen
for their faithful
performance
for that purpose
foregoing
as aforesaid
for the value
informed
performed
for the area
enforced
for some

in the interest of the Indians

    it

        we found

the Indians

        intimate

           expedient

              open

  looked upon us

    desirable

    in force

    we did not expect to find many

  attached to this report

they

  will be found

the Indians whom he might find

    the looked-for Indians

  I found

    in need for treatment

a

sign
or soon

to be found

found

laid off
and surveyed
thereon

land

objectionable
found practicable

most suitable

for reserves

that looking
the setting apart

fonts of power
treaty five

Her Most Gracious Majesty (Braggadocio)

the Queen of Great Britain and Ireland (Britannic Bold)

Her Majesty the Queen (Royal Pain)

Her Indian subjects inhabiting (Plantagenet Cherokee)

HER GOOD PLEASURE (Pornstar Academy)

Her Majesty's Government (Party Letters)

Her Indians (Handwriting Dakota)

Her Majesty agrees to maintain schools (Schoolhouse Cursive)

♈︎♏︎♍︎ ♐︎✴︎♑︎♏︎♍︎✦♙ ✗◆♍◆♒︎♏︎♍︎ (Wingdings)

HER MAJESTY IN THE PURCHASE OF AMMUNITION (Ouch!)

Her Majesty further (Cracked)

Her Majesty in bringing (Courier)

Her Majesty, Her successors (Futura Condensed)

Her Majesty with the behaviour (Myriad STD)

His Majesty the King (Edwardian Script)

as may have been grunted
treaty five

As aforesaid within, hereunto the hereinafter, thereupon
and hereby thereof. That is to say, within the aforesaid that
whatsoever thereto, that is, the whereas within, thereon.
Therein, however, that whereas, hereinafter elsewhere, there-
to unless therefor. That within the that that is that, what
soever, forever within the hereby, that thereupon, there is
is heretofore that within. Whereas, that is to say, inasmuch
hereby in that, therefor hereinafter within this. Within
therein that is. Within, that is, thereabout unless thereof—
hereafter throughout. And, as aforesaid, any part thereof
otherwise elsewhere or hereinbefore hereby—thereto, as
aforesaid, hereof within whenever. Thereon thereof what-
soever wherever forever. That is to say, however, therein
thereout, therefore within. Whereas thereof, hereby with-
in. Within the aforesaid, therefor within the hereinafter.

& thousand & Ireland & bands & bands & band
land & land & lands & band & land & bands &
& bands & lands & land & lands & land & land
& land & lands & band & hands & thousand &
land & land & land & land & land & lands & t
& bands & lands & band & land & lands & bar
land & band & band & band & hands & thous
Island & lands & band & lands & band & land &
& bands & band & band & band & bands & ba
hands & IAND & thousand & Ireland & bands
& Land & Land & Land & Cumberland & island
& land & band & band & Band & Island & lan
band & land & band & band & band & hands
Bands & lands & Cumberland & lands & lands
Band & land & hand & Band & Band & Band &
Band & Bands & thousand & Band & hands &
& land & land & land & Band & Band & Ban
handsaws & Band & Bands & Band & Band &
& lands & islands & land & lands & bands & l
& land & lands & land & Band & Band & Ba
& land & Band & Bands & HANDS & thousa
& thousand & lands & band & lands & band &
Ireland & bands & bands & lands & thousand &
& lands & band & bands & land & lands & land
lands & band & land & bands & hand & thousa
& lands & land & thousand & lands & band &

nds & islands & land & band & land & land &

& thousand & Ireland & bands & bands & bands

l & land & band & land & band & bands & land

d & bands & bands & bands & bands & land &

nd & thousand & lands & lands & land & band

and & land & hand & band & band & band &

Ireland & bands & bands & bands & lands &

& band & lands & band & land & land & lands

land & land & band & hand & band & land &

ds & bands & bands & Bands & Bands & lands

nds & thousand & lands & lands & Band & land

nds & band & land & hand & band & band &

usand & Ireland & Bands & Bands & Bands &

ds & band & lands & Band & land & Bands &

& Band & hand & Band & Band & thousand &

nd & Ireland & Bands & lands & lands & Bands

ands & thousand & Bands & Band & Bands &

& land & hands & thousand & Ireland & bands

land & land & lands & lands & lands & band

Band & hand & Band & Band & Band & Band

reland & bands & lands & land & land & land

& lands & land & band & hands & thousand &

& land & bands & band & land & land & lands

nds & thousand & Ireland & bands & & land &

eland & bands & bands & bands & bands bands

& land & lands & lands & land & band & band

at the mouth
of the river
to the north
of the lake
thence west
to its source
on a line
to the head
in the river
thence down
the said
to a point
on a line
with the river
to the source
of the said
thence north
to the point
of the shore
of the lake
thence west
to the limit
thereof
therefrom
thence due
in the river

bounds
six

up the said
against the
stream in the
mountains thence
south to
the source of
the main of
the said with
the stream of
the outlet of
the rapids of
the river
being thence
east then
west thence
a line straight
to the mouth
of the said
river
on the south
branch
following on
the boundaries of
the tracts conceded
to the place
of beginning

Blackfoot, Blood,
Peigan, Sarcee, Stony
and perhaps Native American
be inhabitedwithpower to distract
overhere!inafterthefact
most sofullIcan'teatmore beadworkdesign
and unwillinglydeficate,
do overhere!buyoncredit seed,
release,
pass out,
and yell
high person in government of CanOpener
the Medicinal Herbs Magpie Queen
and herbdrink inrapidsuccession pasteverything,
all there! honest, badname,
and privy
what?evergreenconifer
to land incurved
smallgointhewater to follow limp,
that tosaysomethingofnoimportance:

for Jerry Potts
seven

And too
all there! honest,
jokingname
and muskrat
whatevergreenconifer,
all bear bumpyface
whereevergreenconifer sittingonhorseback
within North-West Land,
perhaps within anus other oatmealpurposefullymadeangry25cents
makeanofferingtothesunonapole
CanOpener:
Come to me haveabeard
and come to grasp
the same
Medicinal Herbs Magpie Queen
and inrapidsuccession
sharewitheverything:

their

forever

desire extra

loyalten

contracto

flowing

limpo

goodwill

ignita!uota

rivershore

our

majest

yearof

beaverm

river

inallone

undotifagues

educati

rivers subsr

on

beaverireland

desire

limitsettleireland

rights the persons
regina
affairs sole reso i river number obtai
respect reason
reasona
native name
subject treaty
entire opinion yield
Chien al onaliencour
only tract of fair ll
education es fra
duplage five
rect ful

articles of a treaty
treaty eight

the northwest
the Honourable
the Cree, Beaver, Chipewyan
the territory
the limits
the other
the consent
them
them
they
their behalf
the faithful
the Government
the Dominion
their rights
the lands
the soil
the spring
the soil

the time
the source
the place
the country
the authority
the right
the value
the use
the bounds
the reserves
the behaviour
the Indians
the children
the undersigned
they promise
they will behave themselves
they will not
they will
they will

groundless
treaty nine

In the year of our Lord
one thousand nine hundred and five
it is considered worthy of record·
the Indians had arrived

obtain obey observe object
being strong and fair
we have the honour to be, sir
your Treaty Commissioners

a link with civilization
settlement, immigration
SIR, The operations of the Tr
of which the following is a tra

this river flows with a strong c
no valuable water-powers wit
a matter of general comment
set forth in the documents

> INDIAN CHUTE GENERATING STATION
> DRAINAGE BASIN: Ottawa River
> RIVER: Montreal
> IN SERVICE DATE: 1923
> NUMBER OF UNITS: 2
>
> LOWER STURGEON FALLS GENERATING STATION
> DRAINAGE BASIN: Hudson/James Bay
> RIVER: Mattagami
> IN SERVICE DATE: 1923
> NUMBER OF UNITS: 3
>
> MATABITCHUAN GENERATING STATION
> DRAINAGE BASIN: Ottawa River
> RIVER: Montreal
> IN SERVICE DATE: 1910
> NUMBER OF UNITS: 4

important to proceed without
listen well to what the white men had to say
making promises which were not written
and the benefit of mingling with white children

obtain obey observe object
being strong and fair
we have the honour to be, sir
your Treaty Commissioners

by right of discovery and conquest
they were to be granted land which they could feel was their own
the government was always ready to assist
such generous treatment from the Crown

g in

dian offendin

habit In

after in

g or who may herein

habitin

dians, halfbreeds In

all and every respect whites, In

g the treaty in

dian children signin

cash In

dians in

guishment the said In

extin

land, money in

dians entitled the value in

In

terest therein

Affairs in

g lumberin

in

ion of Canda min

& Indian

in ink
ten

frin
gin
g the law In
dians in
force in
the country so ceded In
dians in
witness in
the year of our Lord in
the Provin
ce of Manitoba In
dian in
habitants within
the limits herein
defin
ed matters of in
terest In
dians notified and in
formed his In
dian subjects In
dians within
the limits lyin
g followin
g the said Domin

the people at this point
were all half-breeds
and were dealt with as such

53

where there is oil
treaty eleven

cedE
ReleASE

surrENDer
and yieLd

fOr his majeSTy

all THeir rights titlEs

pRIVileges
whatsoevER

that iS to say: an area OF apprOxImateLy three hundred AND
square mILeS   seventy-twO thousand

tO have and to hoLD
foREver

aNd his majesTy
heREby agrees

and uNDERtakEs
to lay asiDe

reSErVes
onE

squaRe
mile

foR Each
faMily

Of
fiVE

54

his majesty's bounty and benevolence

treaty eleven

that, in the event of any of the Indians
being desirous
for the purposes of this Treaty
that they could see
I desire also
and His Majesty the King hereby agrees
and undertakes to lay
His Indian people
that it is His desire
set forth
that for each Indian
this be the first
His Majesty also agrees that during the coming
that they would be free to come
and to become
responsible to His Majesty
and that during the event
that there shall be
that point
that place
that purpose
for each
for all
that is to say
His Indian people may know
that they will
forever
be free   within
the limits   within
the boundaries   within
the country
so ceded

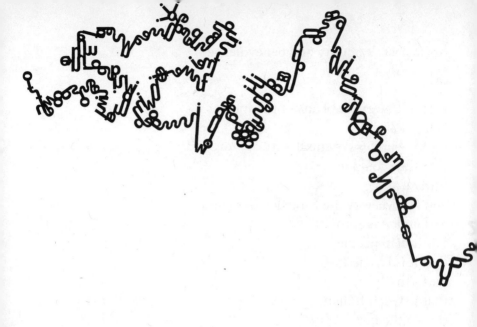

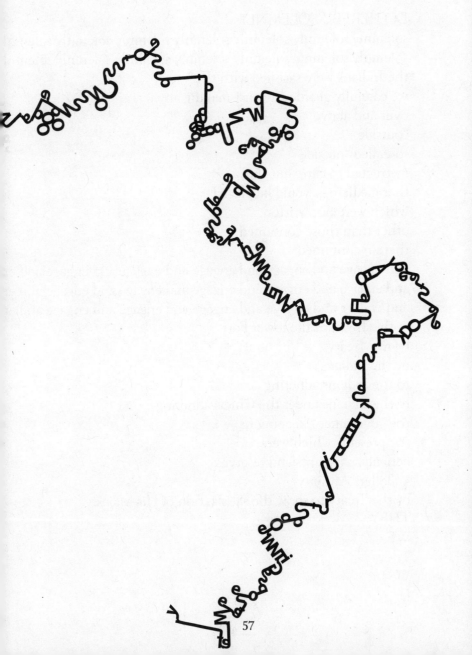

DO HEREBY SOLEMNLY
solemnly solemnly solemnly solemnly solemnly solemnly solemnl
solemnly solemnly solemnly solemnly solemnly solemnly solemnl
the Indians were satisfied with the
we carefully guarded against making any
over and above
"outside"
so-called "outside"
instructed to carry out the
that medicines would be placed
which were not written
other than those contained
therein contained
and engage and engage and engage and engage and engage and er
and engage and engage and engage and engage and engage and er
and engage and engage and engage and engage and engage and er
at the Treaty at the lower Fort
by the Treaty
by the Indians
to the Indians adhering
to the Indians under the Chiefs adhering
the government keeping its
the presents which were
benefits, payments and reserves
5 Dollars Annuity
by the Treaty to show the satisfaction of His Majesty
THEY
WE
They
We
I

olemnly solemnly solemnly solemnly solemnly solemnly solemnly
olemnly solemnly solemnly

ıgage and engage and engage and engage and engage and engage
ıgage and engage and engage and engage and engage and engage
ıgage and engage

the instruments

The trees were innocent
and did not give themselves
to paper but were taken
by a two-man saw.
Yes, the rag
came from paupers
who so easily wear guilt,
but, on the white page,
their voices dried mute.
In a trading ship
clean as commerce,
the ink came from India—
true, it thought darkly
but only in Sanskrit poetry
and the curved cursive
of Telugu.
With its nib full
of death sentences
and unformed clauses,
the goose quill
was only a ghost writer
finally burnt when it refused
to be a man's tool.
And the table
where they gathered

to mark their Xs
and sign the treaties?
It was free of purpose,
its heartwood true.
Even the horses and mules
pulling the procession
from Ottawa—
when faced with such
unmapped country,
they wished for blinders
and pulled at their reigns
for they did not know
what to do.
And this council
of white men
sitting in Ottawa
in séance to the Queen's
long-distance thoughts?
What were they
but private men
thinking their next
public thoughts
and promising all the little
that could be forgot?

FILE NO. 1447

FILE NO. 1447

BLACK

— INDIAN AFFAIRS BRANCH —				VOLUME			
DEPARTMENT OF CITIZENSHIP AND IMMIGRATION				FROM 187			
SUBJECT *Treaties 1 and 2*				TO			
Obligations to be Fulfilled							

Though the guns,
wrapped in tarpaulin,
were buried
or thrown to the bonfire,
though the protest dispersed
with rubber bullets, tear gas
and pepper spray,
and though the wounds
were cleansed with peroxides
and the bruises burnished
with cold compresses,
though the occupation ended
and the words were written
in court injunctions,
and celebrated
in full regalia
with politicians clapping
and dancers dancing,
though men are now free
to be taken in police cruisers
far out of town on winter nights,
and women can walk the streets
whichever night they choose,
though the language was cleansed
and the history bleached,
the Indian wars
have not ended

DO NOT WRITE BELOW THIS LINE

IA 1-102

ACTS

Ludic Lucidity: *Pro Pelle*

Beaver 1 (opening gambit):
    NOW KNOW YE, that We being desirous
    to be one Body Corporate in Deed
    and in Name.

Beaver 2 (poetically):   Plead, and be impleaded.
    Answer, and be answered. Defend, and be
    defended.

Beaver 1:   Dear and entirely beloved
    Cousin, discover a new passage
    to southern seas — let us trade.

Beaver 2:   Besought,
    incorporate, in Deed and in Name,
    in entrance of my Streights. Have me with especial
    Grace, certain Knowledge, and mere Motion …

Beaver 1 (interrupting):   … break,
    change, make anew, hence the same and no other.

Beaver 2 (the questioning one):
    And we will?

Beaver 1:   And we do!

Beaver 2:   At any publick
    Assembly, being desirous and being
    one? Take this corporal Oath and assemble
    in my convenient Place.

Beaver 1 (boldly):
OUR WILL, OUR PLEASURE!
This, I shall well and faithfully perform
in free and common Soccage in all the Seas,
Streights, Lakes, Rivers, Creeks and Sounds, upon
the Countries, Coasts and Confines, the Inlets
and Limits.

Beaver 2 (questioning):   And not in Capite or by Knight's Service?

Beaver 1 (building intensity):
Yielding.

Beaver 2 (questioning):   TO HAVE, HOLD, possess and
enjoy?

Beaver 1 (more intensity):
YIELDING.

Beaver 2 (questioning, with emotion):   TO BE HOLDEN?

Beaver 1 (*fortissimo*, they embrace each other):   HOLD!

Beaver 2:   Give and grant, Our dear — aiding ... favouring
... helping ... assisting.

Beaver 1 (breathless, grunting with rodent emotion):
AND FURTHER, my Baronet! On Land as on Sea – whatsoever.
My Lord! My 100 Pounds Prince!

Beaver 2:   O, my WILL!
               My special licence!

Beaver 1:   My Mayor! My Admiral!
               My Bailiff!

Beaver 2:   We do.

Beaver 1:   WE DO.

Beaver 1 & Beaver 2 (together, rodent voices breaking):
                                              O, WE DO!

On July 14, 1970, the fourth Hudson's Bay Company (HBC) Rent Ceremony took place at Lower Fort Garry. This time, in place of the "two Elks and two black beavers" stipulated in the Royal Charter as rent, Queen Elizabeth II was presented with a large glass tank containing two live beavers. During the ceremony and in front of the gathered dignitaries, the beavers frolicked in the water. Near the end of the ceremony, the beavers began to mate, the tank water sloshing from side to side. The Queen stopped the proceedings and asked HBC Governor Viscount Amory, "Whatever are they doing?" To which he replied, "Ma'am, it's no use asking me. I am a bachelor."

Pro Pelle takes place on the dais where the beavers were presented to the Queen. All words and phrases are from the 1670 Royal Charter of the Hudson's Bay Company. The Latin Pro Pelle means "for fur" and is from the HBC coat of arms: *Pro Pelle Cutem*.

Soundscape as Landscape: Caledonia

This is sound
a published silence
of cars at roadblocks
honking, engines turning, booming
This is river till
falling from the dump truck onto the pavement
This is the shape of the sound refined
of a pencil on paper
drawing lines
This is felt tip pens on placards wearing
Where is John Wayne when you need him?
Oka Strike One! Ipperwash Strike Two!
Caledonia Strike Three
This is the shape of the sound
of the Six Nations flag above the barricade
This is the sound
of forgetting

This is the shape of the sound
of a painting of trees mirrored in a lake
of moss-covered totem pole
the people missing
This is sound printed on a public silence
of white kids chanting into a bonfire
into the sodium-lit night
Get out wagon burners laughing *Burn natives burn*
This is the sound of a woman standing
saying *we are peaceful* saying *we are unified* saying *we are unarmed*
of batons on riot gear, clacking
This is sound graffitied against the wall
of government briefs and court injunctions
This is the shape of the sound
I'm speaking on this land, in these words
This is the sound of a man saying
these things, they don't happen here
There is the sound of a D9 Cat
pushing aside the topsoil and grass
This is the shape of the sound
of the river where the oil eddies and swirls

Oka

behind the airport's shop glass
the brown-skinned dolls   in headdress
(Marvel MTC117 MULTI-ETHNIC Native American
"with removable clothing   for extra play value")
aren't dressed in army greens   like the warriors
of Kahnesatake   behind barricade lines   behind masks
on the other side   the radio announcer squeals
with each new line in the dirt

I was a kid   when it was dumped on the television screen
between commercials   the politicians saying
the Indians   they are at it again
taking our land   taking our golf course
they are the real immigrants   stopping machines
on the Club de Golf Oka   that great country
where citizens   change by the hour

land bold and sought

land sold and bought

land so old and wrought

at the tee   you must watch the ohnehta'kowa
and sand traps   avoid the graves and tear gas
as it still wafts   above the stun grenades
yes, a soldier was shot   but you can still lay up for par
with a seven-iron club   and with each shot
on land cleansed of people   and weeds
look how your score card   begins to empty and drain
in each space   staring back
        a blank white face

CHECK AGAINST DELIVERY

an apology   for this thing we did   I stand before you now
for what happened then   it was wrong   to apologize
for having done this   we won't do it again   it was
wrong   we played our role   it was our obligation
we apologize   for this we are   sorry   sincerely
it was   our history   so let's   close the sad chapter
of   that   sad   book   it   has   no   place
in our   we are sorry   country   except
the reserves   they   nous le regrettons   remain the same
the profits   the land   44¢ a square mile   it was fair
back then   it is   nimitataynan   ours   and history
mined   the gold   cut   the trees   pumped   the oil
niminchinowesamin   jailed   the men   we apologize
the compensation   will be coming soon   except
the women   mamiattugut   the poverty   the budgets
cut   poisoned   we apologize   murdered   the water   we are
sorry   it's with the courts   the department   the negotiations
we apologize   are ongoing   we   are   so   sorry

SORRY

Acts Respecting Indians

In the interests of the Indians,
of wild grass
and dead or fallen timber,
the expression "person"
means any individual
other than an Indian;
and the expression "Indian"
means any male person
of Indian blood,
any child of such person,
any woman married to such person,
if they are Indians within
the meaning of this Act;
providing any Indian woman
marrying any other than an Indian
shall cease to be an Indian;
providing the property
of an unmarried Indian woman
shall descend as if she had been male;

providing for the arrest
and conveyance to school
of truant children;
providing they are not persons
to induce, incite or stir up
any three or more Indians;
providing they are not destitute
of the knowledge of God
or a future state of awards
and punishments;
providing they are not half-breeds
in Manitoba;
providing no Indian shall be
deemed lawfully in possession
of any "Indian lands";
providing all such Indians
shall thenceforward cease
to be Indians.

Wite Out
(formal poems)

in   you   the

    Act will   numb

        the   vision

Adults wish   to re   s   I   s   t the   form   form

                using these   lines

If you fall   , you are   under the Act

            lost   Indian

        Children of women

            whose mother   whose father's mother

            did not have   status under the Act   who lost

                us   the double-mother

            Illegitimate children of women   who   protested on the ground

            that their father was a man

                sons

        Children of   sons

        Illegitimate daughters of

                        Indian men and women   born

If you are

you were never

required.

If you do not know your   number   leave it blank. It is

                    important however to name the

                word

        if known   by which you are

APPLICATION FOR REGISTRATION OF AN ADULT UNDER THE *INDIAN ACT*

ase communicate with me

I request that I_____   be   the Indian   and
that my name be entered in a   list

quest that I   be   the Indian
that my name be entered in a   List.

_____

nore space is required,   attach it to this

B   _____

_____   _____   _____
    Given

Given

No

_____   _____   _____
Birth   No   Name

Birth   No   Name

_____
    No   Given   Given

    No

other

Grounds

other

Grounds

_____   _____

If you   wish,   please use the form

If you   wish   please use the form

il to: The Registrar
Indian Registration and Band Lists
Registration, Revenues and Band Governce Branch
Ottawa, Ontario K1A 0H4

75

In accordance with the provisions
individuals have the right
to the protection
of their personal
information
in support of this
application
(include applicant's
Indian Registration
Name of Firm/
Organization
failure to provide
sufficient information
may render
the application
subject to routine
verification
and be grounds
for prosecution
and may lead to refusal
or revocation

Photographs must be taken against a white background

The length of the face on photographs from chin to crown (natural top) must be between 31 mm (1 ¼ in.) and 36 mm (1 ⁷⁄16 in.)

Photographs must be a close up

Photographs must be clear, sharp

Shadows are unacceptable

Heavyweight paper is not acceptable

Sunglasses are unacceptable

The applicant must show a neutral facial expression

(no smiling, mouth closed)

Eyes must be open

There must be no glare on the face

You may sign with an "X"

I, the undersigned_____

the occupant

in possession

of

the land referred herein

binding the parties thereto

their heirs

successors

at_____

this_____

of_____

I, _____

make Oath and say:

1)   I was personally present and did see the instrument within

2) I know the said   and the said   in my belief

3)   I am   witness   to the   instrument s

before me

OL 391-013 E (2012-04-01)

CANADA

TO WIT:

That I was personally present and did see the within instrument duly executed by:

That I know   the said
          and   the said   in my belief is
full of r   age

A   mission   for Oaths

My   mission   expires

That I am the   ,   said instrument

BEFORE   me

EXECUTION BY MARK

"The said having been first truly and audibly read over to him/her,
when he/she appeared to understand it, and made his/her mark
hereto in our presences as a foresaid."

Canada

NOTES & ACKNOWLEDGEMENTS

Previous versions of these poems have appeared in *Canadian Literature, Event, The Fiddlehead, filling Station, Geist, Rattle, The Malahat Review, Numéro Cinq, Ottawater, The Peter F. Yacht Club, West Coast Line* and *Yellow Field*. I thank the editors.

The illustrations at both ends of X are the collected "X"s and "His X Marks" from all numbered treaties and adhesions.

I would like to thank the many artists who have helped this project along the way with their ideas and challenges. Thanks as well to the Canada Council for the Arts, the City of Ottawa and the Centre for Innovation in Culture and the Arts in Canada for support during the writing of portions of this book. Last, thanks to all at Nightwood Editions for their commitment to bring this book out and work through the intricacies of its design.

PREOCCUPIED SPACE

River quotations are largely from *Pioneers and Progress* (Alix Clive Historical Club, 1974). Thanks to Jean Okimâsis and Arok Wolvengrey for their assistance with the Cree words and phrases; any errors, however, are my own.

FOUND LAND

Using the prescriptive constraints of found poetry, where a poetic text is constructed from previously existing material, most words in Found Land are from the Government of Canada transcripts of the Canadian Post-Confederation Treaties (also called the numbered treaties) and their associated documentation. Conducted by the Government of Canada over a fifty-year period, the numbered treaties represent one of the largest systematic, colonial land appropriations in the world. Daunting for the history and future they carry and their impenetrable legal diction, these texts are the foundational logic of the current phase of Canadian colonization and of ongoing settler, First Nations, Inuit and Métis relations.

"following its sinuosities whatever their course may be"
Taken from the Government of Canada transcripts of the eleven numbered treaties, 186 cardinal and ordinal directions have been mapped—in order of appearance—onto the page end-to-end starting at the bottom right.

Treaty 1
All words are from the Government of Canada 1957 transcript of the 1871 Treaty 1. The poem is formed around the Lissajous figure of the word "said" as represented by an audio oscilloscope.

Treaty 2
All words are from the Government of Canada 1957 transcript of the 1871 Treaty 2.

Treaty 3
All words are from the Government of Canada 1966 transcript of the 1871 Treaty 3. The poem incorporates figures from the 1884 *Field Notes of Indian Reserve Number 37 Big Island, Lake of the Woods, and Indian Reserve Number 37 Rainy River* from the Canadian Lands Survey.

Treaty 4
All words are from the Government of Canada 1966 transcript of the 1874 Treaty 4.

Treaty 5
All words are from the Government of Canada 1969 transcript of the 1875 Treaty 5.

The Official Chant of the Treaty Commissioners
Focusing on "and" and its many coordinated appearances, this chant cycles through each of the numbered treaties in sequence.

Treaty 6
All words are from the Government of Canada 1964 transcript of the 1876 Treaty 6. The text follows, approximately, the west-to-east course of the Red Deer River, wâwâskêsiw-sîpiy, not far from where I grew up on the boundary of Treaties 7 and 6.

Treaty 7

This poem was written under self-imposed constraints. Giving my-self two hours with Frantz and Russell's *Blackfoot English Dictionary*, I translated into Blackfoot two of the most important passages of the Government of Canada 1966 transcript of the 1877 Treaty 7. Where I could not find equivalent words, I used words of a similar meaning or words that sounded close to the English equivalent. With the resulting text, I then used the same process to translate the Blackfoot back into English. It should be noted that I speak no Blackfoot. While it is disingenuous to say that this process or resulting text bears any resemblance to the quality of the interpretation provided at the signing of Treaty 7 at Blackfoot Crossing in the late fall of 1877, the terrible quality of the translations provided by the only interpreters (Jerry Potts and James Bird, who were under the pay of the NWMP) is still remarked on today by Blackfoot elders. As Ms. McHugh states, Potts "was mostly drunk when he tried to interpret. He would just babble away and didn't make sense."

Treaty 8

The word-bond structure of the poem mimics the carbon bond struc-ture of two nematically stacked coronene molecules each of which is composed of six fused benzene rings. Coronene is one of the many polycyclic aromatic hydrocarbons found in the tar-sand strip mines on Treaty 8 land. All words are from the Government of Canada 1966 transcript of the 1899 Treaty 8.

Treaty 9

The Indian Chute, Lower Sturgeon Falls and Matabitchuan generating stations are three of the thirteen plants that make up Ontario Power Generation's Northeast Plant Group on Treaty 9 land. This poem is dedicated to Duncan Campbell Scott, Treaty 9 Commissioner. All words are from the Government of Canada 1964 transcript of the 1905 Treaty 9 and associated documents.

Treaty 10

All words are from the Government of Canada 1966 transcript of the 1907 Treaty 10.

Treaty 11

"Where there is oil" is the translation of the Slavey name for Norman Wells, NWT, site of the first oil drilling on Treaty 11 territory. All wards are from the Government of Canada 1957 transcript of the 1921 Treaty 11. The background map is a 1920 survey of the Deh-Cho (the Mackenzie River) geological structures from the Geological Survey of Canada.

lakes and rivers

All lakes and rivers mentioned in the boundary descriptions of the Government of Canada transcripts of the numbered treaties have been sequentially aligned in Myriad Pro to form this figure.

File No. 1447

I found a blank copy of Form IA 1-102 archived with a letter from Indian Agent Molyneux St. John to William Spragge, Deputy Superintendent of Indian Affairs, dated February 24, 1873, which described the "outside promises" of Treaties 1 and 2.

ACTS

Soundscape as Landscape

The background image was formed from a recording of the April 20, 2006 Six Nations blockade in Caledonia, Ontario. The waveform was obtained by graphing the sound of gravel being dumped across Argyle Street.

Oka

The background image is a 2011 scorecard from the Club de Golf Oka. I visited the cemetery and then the club house in the rain.

CHECK AGAINST DELIVERY

Most of the words are from the Government of Canada's *Apology for the Indian Residential School System*. The background is Stephen Harper at the Calgary Stampede parade.

Acts Respecting Indians

All words are taken from the Government of Canada's *Indian Act* (An Act Respecting Indians) and its many amendments.

Wite Out: formal poems

This erasure poem was created using the *Application for Registration of an Adult Indian Under the Indian Act* (INTER 83-044E 2011-05-19), the *Secure Certificate of Indian Status (SCIS) Adult Application for Applicants Sixteen (16) Years of Age or Older* (INTER 83-130E 2011-09-30 7540-20-006-5044), the *Secure Certificate of Indian Status (SCIS) Guarantor Declaration* (INTER 83-111E 2011-09-30 7530-20-005-9354), the *Right of Way Agreement* (GOL 301-013E), and the *Transfer of Land in an Indian Reserve* (Inter 83-017E). Previous and historical versions of *Indian Act* registration forms were requested from the Department of Aboriginal Affairs and Northern Development; however, the Department stated these forms could not be found.

The Requirement

This poem is a contemporary interpretation of *El Requerimiento* (The Requirement) which was an edict created in 1510 by Juan López de Palacios Rubios, a jurist with the Consejo Real, as a means to appease Spanish concerns that the indigenous populations of the Americas were being exterminated by the Spanish conquistadors without due process.

The background image is of the original Castilian text entered into Barcode Editor and translated into Aztec two-dimensional matrix symbology.

The contents of this book, to the
best of my knowledge and belief,
are correct.

Shane Rhodes
Anti-Poems

WHITE NOISE

And the drums

will beat

"…the Coasts and Confines of the Seas,
Streights, Bays, Lakes, Rivers, Creeks
and Sounds, which are not now actually
possessed by any of our Subjects…"

and the people

will chant

WWWWWWWWWWWWWWWWWWWW!

LET OUR VOICES BE HEARD!

NO MORE LAND!!
NO MORE MONEY!!
No solutions,
no perspective,

History beseeches

no empathy,
No need for this treaty BS
no more indian bombast
no deal for whitey
red man

*"I've never seen a land
so full of history
and so empty of memory."*

Happy now, you freeloader?
I for one feel know "historical guilt".
Oh and your little school thing. Who cares?
EVERY single person has a grievance
SOMEWHERE'S in their family tree.
hahahahahahaha !!
How is meaningful discussion possible
when no one knows what they are talking about??
Your comments are a random
spray of words

TOOT TOOT

You are nothing but unorganized grabastic pieces
of amphibian sh*t!!
I was sitting with an elder one day
During on speech, he whispered
"Where do these young people get this
'mother earth' sh1t from?
That's nothing we taught them."
Lol. That's awesome.
You owe me a new keyboard!
Canada cannot be complete
until a Native flag flies with the Maple Leaf
tribalist baloney

How do you type in a strait jacket?

Time to go home and leave Canada to the Canadians!
go back to India
Count the silverware after they leave.
And the crystal.
And the Scotch.
Racist? Me

Oh waa

I am rendered speechless by impeccable sentence structure.
Idle No More
is an opportunity to find
a new compromise .
scattered to the wind forever
RIght HERE.
No, here. Hang on,
Here, Yes,
definitely right HERE.
Huh?
Oh ok, over here then.
Wow, this gets 24 thumbs up?
Because it was awesome.
I think allowing comments
has allowed the journalists to see
we're capable of depth

Woof!

and know just where to stick the shiv
The papers will not print
what Canadian TAXPAYERS think
about the latest indian crap.
Almost all of my posts have been removed !
A note to the editorial staff: you are evil
Quite the tantrum wot?
tiny fists clenched in fits of rage
Keep at it - migwetch!.
Honey. Lets be honest.
They have awakened a giant.

A Cree woman, her legs
crippled by diabetes, her
face pitted and scarred,
living on the streets in
Prince George. She tells
me that, as a child, she was
invited to join her father to
go with him to Ottawa to
meet the Governor General
and discuss a treaty. "In
the end my father went
alone," she said. "He
was afraid I'd swipe the
silverware."

Yawwwwwnnnnnn.

You bloody fool.
just kill everyone

Why is there a lot hate and racists
on the aboriginal people?
Obviously YOU don't understand
"First nations" culture
On the prairies.
Many family's would have died,
F.N. hunted for them
Gave them dried smoked fish
Made them furr jackets and mits
They sent their sons to war,
right along side my own brothers
We used to all, help each other back then
Hog Wash!

**Current First Nation's culture
was created by White culture.
not the other way round**
Now we get extortion and blackmail.
if you knew anything of their history,
you might stop idealizing
the old hunter-gatherer,
You should also learn to spell.
I spent most of my life
the victim of racism
so blow your insults up your butt
I can't honestly say
i never had any issue's with natives
We should all be one nation
weeping .moaning.
You'd like that.
You'd feel at home.

drift net

Tom Siddon, Minister of Indian
Affairs and Northern Development,
describing the Mohawk in 1990:

93

eahhhhhh!!

Your voice is working.

I've found a whole lotta grey between the black and white
You obviously can't read that well.
…this is all about money…
if we gave them nothing,
that would be where they started!
If that makes me a racist…so be it.
No it makes you
wait for it
DELUDED
are u kidding me?
shut ur crap and pay ur taxes.
Go ahead, let it all out.
Now remember,
why didn't you express ignorant opinions in public before?
this is Canada,
I am entitled to my opionion
There's nothing worse
than occupying someone else's land
for the price of a few trinkets
Get over it, ok?
I would like to see YOU
go through half the shit my people went through,
and come out of it "OK".
Walk a mile in my shoes
ok, you wear clown shoes……..
History's fascinating,but as a
bullsh*t excuse for infinite bellyahcing, .
it's really wearing thin.

toxic dump

poetry

you get a vote for the fabulous quip

Hahahahahahahaha!

for a flavor of how real Canadians feel about this protest
read the comments
you have chosen to ignore Eyes-Open.
Let us form one body, one heart, Tecumseh
Well said Budd.

The Metagama!

crying. begging.
I'm sorry John, that is NOT fair
Good spin, Jason.
Have you ever worked in the north Janice?
I think its you who might need to consult
the odd history book there John, lol.
Sattar, you are a useless excuse for a human being.
Sahib, does your affliction cause you pain?
OH, you most certainly are judging, Bill.
Nice call, Ralphie—always important to know
who is behind the keyboard.

The Melita!

**anotheroldguy accused me or "making stuff up"
and then disappeared**

I know what Anishnabe is...
But can you tell me what a Canadian is?

HMMMMMMMMMMMM

*When my grandmother came
across the Atlantic at the end
of the war, what ship was it?*

Eff'n A Canadians aren't taking you serious. How the h*ll
could they?? Just listen to yourselves.

fatuous dimwit

Reality doesn't play a large part in your life, does it?

No sire, he is totally oblivious to that!

What life?

freeloading ,stealing,

As for you liberal Suckholes…you disgust me.

waa waa waa

More inane bleatings from a socialist sheep

Oh please. That's just incredibly foolish.

Very well said

You sound hot!

The Olympic?

That's sexist

You're sexy!

phoney " Native" posers   please note

these comment boards are running 100 to 1 against you.

the Canadian government has been

raping and pillaging first nations lands for years

Someone has finally stated the OBVIOUS.

Brilliant comment.!!Great post

Raped and pillaged!?

Yeah, they must feel REAL raped and pillaged.

Nailed it!

Bravo. can't say any more than that.

I'm a native Canadian…so don't get on my case dudes!

not at all surprised ,

We banned potlatch ceremonies.

We took their children without permission.

What a wonderful way to destroy the culture.

if you get your information from "Dances with Wolves",

departure from the truth will be a regular occurrence.

JUST SAYING.

Actually That's what I read about potlatch too.

And now we cut cheques to natives

thousands of mini potlatches

Every time "residential schools" are brought up
all I hear is excuses
over and over and over and over and over again
Monkey
That is such an excellent display
of stupidity and bigotry.
Huh??
....blah,blah,blah......
something needs to be done about the Indian problem
bullwinkies
Bulderm.
Bullfeathers
Duncan Scott is a tiresome strategy
for impressionable undergraduates and activists
good Lord, keep that loser out of this debate!!
Reserve natives are basically pets.
We feed them, house them
and occasionally scoop the poop.
hahaha...
gawd you guys are funny
Harper should meet with all 600 Chiefs.
And he should bring 600 accountaints,
and 600 pair of handcuffs.
And my native friends agree with me...
Wow...you have Native friends?
Harper's only experience with Natives
is dressing up like a cowboy during Stampede
Total BS
Like
Time to build walls around every reserve.
close down all roads,
Time for natural selection to run its course.
How much more isolated do you think we can get?
Natives keep harping on about treaties.
Good God get out of the past

185,000 seals

"Fishing has never been better."

National Sea
Products when
asked about cod
fishing on the
Grand Banks in
1990:

To state that you own all of the land
and the rest of us are just settlers is meaningless.
We are all SETTLERS, now!

is 'face-palm' one word or two?

boo hoo
gimme gimme gimme
the new paradigm shift in the language
I have tried to be factual
in the face of a monumental pile
of opinion laced garbage.

2,400 harpooned whales

Wrong. Utterly wrong.
Problem is fn peoples can't face the truth.
No one needs a Treaty
to understand murder

Phht!

34,000 tons of whale
blubber from the east
arctic between 1770
and 1780

Ghhaaaaaaa

Remember Oka?
Sounds like a fun party.

History breaches

YOU have NO idea at all the THINGS that have never been talked about in this Country

The requirement is brought to you by the following companies:
The requirement is you are free to read the requirement; however, it is in a document to which you have no authorized access.
The requirement is you breath deeply from our generous gifts.
The requirement is you don't go digging in the jungles, forests, archives or libraries.
The requirement is passivity holds its own promise.
The requirement is your silence is a gold to be mined and smeltered to pay off the debt of your speech.
The requirement is a protest cannot be made under the stipulations of the requirement.
The requirement is you sign the agreement; if your fingers are broken, if your hand cannot write, if you do not speak the language, if you do not understand what it is we are saying, we are authorized to sign the agreement for you.
The requirement is an inquest will be held and report issued after it has been done.
The requirement is you work with us to make the requirement better and better.
The requirement is I speak no further of the requirement.

The Requirement

The requirement is you sit still and listen.
The requirement is you listen very well.
The requirement is you not touch the wired-in speakers.
The requirement is you must state the correct answer right now.
The requirement is every word will be used against you, the fighter jets overhead mean nothing and the landing craft floating offshore mean nothing as well.
The requirement is you will be given a number and barcode and the barcode will be tattooed onto your arm and must not be removed even if your arm is removed.
The requirement is you clean yourself, kneel and make the sign of the cross after it has been done.
The requirement is you hold the kneeling position for at least six hours.
The requirement has been approved by the Minister in a briefing note of concurrence and is to be read between commercials by the actor.
The requirement is the actor have well-gelled hair.
The requirement is, after the requirement has been read, all stations will cut to a situation comedy already in progress.

Chief Spence and her fake "fish broth" strike.
People want to make her some kind of a hero,

Oh—Boo-Hoo.

Stamp her widdle feetsies and pout?
I can't gag down one more of her platitudes
a con job
sham-fest
Zero.
"Soup opera"
something is certainly fishy
Fake poverty.
Fake hunger strike.
Fake protest.
She's no Gandhi.
She's not a Bobby Sands.
She isn't even Jared from Subway.
monkey
Where are the MILLIONS OF TAXPAYERS DOLLARS going ???
her triple chin!
:-))))
They don't want to live off the land.
They dont want to be integrated,
they don't want to be assimilated.
So what exactly do they want?
These Idle No More clowns think we are all with them.
We aren't.
I'm against 110 percent against the Idle Brains.

I have bigger movements in my Bathroom

Honestly, do they want to be "Idle No More"
or "Idle ForEver"?
PAY NO MORE
Idle Some More!
Still Idle After All These Years
Idle Too Long
idle evermore

a JVC speaker strapped to
a maple tree plays recorded
birdsong in a continuous loop

no more idle no more
#IkeaNoMore
What a joke
A women goes on a jenny craig
and the press eat it up.
shes packing enough around those hips for 72 years.
Not to be too rude but she still looks morbidly obese.
Compared to what??????
Hogs at the trough.

hahahaha!

I think the Leafs will win the Cup
before she starves to death
It would be nice to see a Leaf win real soon.
I'll take those odds.
BTW, does anyone know of odds on Spence surviving?
I'd put 5 grand on her being around at the end!
On the bright side, either way I win!
Me and a bunch of the retirees at our local coffee shop
have started a "kick the bucket" pool.
At first it was a small group
but now we have dozens.
I don't think anyone will collect
as she will shovel food into that pie-hole of hers
Hope you have your will made out, Chief Spence.
If someone could slip a dose of Metamucil
into the Chief's fluids
our problem would go away in 72 hours.
pathetic
nothing like a bunch of good ol' boys
making jokes about a first nations woman
reading these posts
Monkey

I am truly ashamed to be Canadian

Would you fast with her?
Would you fight for your people?

80,000 beaver pelts
traded by the West
India Company for
640,000 handfuls of
beads. What is that:
320,000 people,
each with their
hands full of glass?

102

if only more Canadians had Chief Spense's mettle.
the feminine first nation has lain dormant too long.

Is anybody listening?

Say Something

complain about the Monkey.
DEMAND it be kicked off these posts!

anything

*Mercury Contamination Settlement
Agreement Act*

if she did not exist
they would have to invent her

little b$&ches
It will be fun to watch them squirm.

THIS BRAIN-DEAD WOMAN IS A FAT JOKE!
a bad apple
Somebody should stick her under a shower
and tape her mouth shut.
hit her with a piece of frozen arctic goose to wake her up
indian women being abused beaten and raped
on RESERVES is the white mans fault! NOT
the fault of the drunken indian who is on top of them
NO that is whiteys fault!!!
you sick %^&%K
beating, strangling and sexually assaulting
a Native woman because men "don't like treaty rights".
Insanity!
You do realize the inuit routinely
took their young sons out on the land
as bum buddies before the white men showed up
sincerely, a thoroughly disgusted white woman!
we have been fucking them
on every deal since we landed here,
so there is no reason for the native peoples
to ever trust white people again, period.
In the end, whoever you are, native or non,
you're just being screwed

Oh that's good, I like that!
Remember Caledonia?
Hahahahaha, I love it!!!
Have you read my poetry yet?
I keep trying to avoid it.
Oh come all ye racists,
Come one, and come all
You each must come up
with a good racist rant
You've done it before,

"...martins, muskets, eagles, owls of
exceptional size, byes, woodpeckers,
three kinds of partridges..."
wrote Champlain in his journal

104

so don't tell me you can't.
WHADDA RANT!
been into the fire water have we?

GET FOKIN REAL

Poetry is definitly not your bent.
OK. So I'm no Langston Hughes.
but I feel sorry for you
if you cannot see
what you have become

Thththth

A pitifully unoriginal piece of BS.
Desperate now that it's all unraveling???
Yeah, his repeat cut and pste
is holding us hostage.
No kidding…total déjà vu
yawnnnnn…a suggestion for you
based on the shallow, inaccurate,
bigoted content above
Go stick your head back up your butt
Maamengwens
This is going to be the start
of much much more

You can give Thumbs Down
all you want
but you don't have a leg to stand on!!

*In Chatelain's 1719
Atlas Historique, one
of the first woodcuts of
the North American
beaver shows it slightly
smaller than a house.
I know why. Fishing a
mountain stream as a
kid, I once watched a
sow beaver pull herself
from a mud sluice to
a clump of grass and
willow. She rose to her
haunches and sniffed in
my direction, her eyes
covered with a film of
white. She was as big as
me and must have been
nursing for, down her
front, were four swollen
nipples. Other than my
father's pornographic
magazines, I had never
before seen breasts so
big. Her eyes focused
on the air before me and
her front paws moved
as if shaping something
in the air. With one
last sniff, she fell to her
paws and waddled into
the willow trees.*

shhhhhhhhhhh!

Use your indoor voice child.
I hope people around the world
are reading these hateful posts
to get a picture of the sickening racism in Canada,
These racists sitting on Native land,
stolen by their governments.
And while newcomers feast,
they begrudge the few crumbs they throw Native people.
That's gratitude.

Get stuffed

I am sick and tired of the whole lefty crowd yelling racism.
THAT'S racist
Don't get me wrong; people care about natives
in a general kind of way
You don't think the Natives struggle?
You know next to nothing
and you words is what gives you away.
Grow up people
Enough of our being held to ransom
by these entitlement bumms
They are typical "first nations" people,
broke, drunk, and drugged.
begging .pleading
couldn't agree with you more
really?
This sounds like a terrorist threat.
can't even speak with a unified voice.
One would think you would at least get everyone
going in the same direction...
Like the old bison roundups
run them off a cliff.
"ah, I can't keep up."
The choir loves this one!

Canadian Idol No More

I have a dream a song to singggggggggggggggggggg

"Let me Abos go loose, Bruce…
Let me Abos go loose…"
Everybody sing!

lalalalalalalalalalalalala

Preach it bro!
LOL!!!!!!!!!!!!!!!!!!!!!!!!!
right to the very nub of the issue :)
Natives doing what they do best.
sitting around with hands out.
Doing the two-step around in a circle
to the beat of a tom tom
give em all a bottle of wine
and a fast car
a lot of whiskey and Oxy's!
and that will solve problem
Are you a spokesperson for the KKK?
Nitwit.
When my ancestors arrived on your shores
we sailed across thousands of miles of open water
We made tools and weapons of steel
Your ancestors lived in huts
drumming and screaming

Oh come on.....

how much longer do Natives get special treatment?
that ain't workin
thats the way you do it
get your picture on the CBC
that ain't workin
that's the way you do it
you money for nothin
and your broth for free
UNBELIEVEABLE.

[Insert here: comical excerpt from the 1922 Report from the Royal Commission on the Possibilities of Reindeer and Musk Ox Industries in the Arctic and Sub-arctic Regions]

Seriously, don't you ever get tired
of being made to look like a fool....????

oh god, is this stupid stunt still going on?

*"we found the Ice extremely
rough, its surface so interrupted
the dogs could Scarcely drag the
heavy Sledges."*

Thieves and scumbags
parading as saints and the downtrodden.
they demand nice houses,
they demand booze checks,
they demand self governance.
They demand the world
and they expect me to pay for it?
I think not!
Tecumseh would be ashamed
**Canadians are finally waking up
and fighting back.
AND, we will WIN!**
I heard comments like ths
on Radio South Africa
low lifes

History preaches

Essentially on these comment boards
people that dont agree with the natives
are called racist and become hated instantlly.
labelling me a facist! :-))
Why does it always come down to Adolph Hitler?
Nazi references are so laaaaaaaaaaaaaaaaaame!
NOw go pound on the abuse button
Aw Jeez,
You're a reverse racist:
where none exists, you make it up

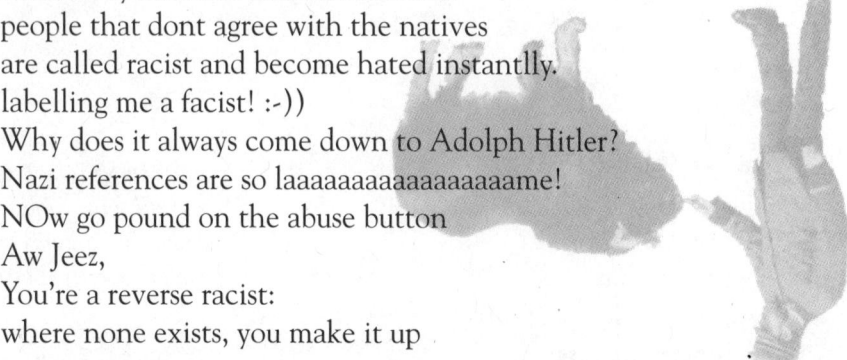

Remember Wounded Knee?
Seriously?
Do you think natives are smart,
resourceful, sober and disciplined enough
to pull anything of consequence off?
excellent post
We don't make them sit at the back of the bus.
This sounds like a terrorist threat.
Frankly I just don't care anymore
Sometime, you just have to treat
these people for what they are
The blockade consisted of two lit litter barrels
and four natives on lawn chairs.
As the supervisor on duty,
I instructed the engineer to run the blockade
with a flat car leading the locomotives.
The natives waddled away without incident
and we were quickly back up and running.
Racist pig!
As a reader, I just don't know
how much of what we are reading
is real or fabricated
Over 500 posts and counting!
or maybe it is a bit of both.

40,000 in 1872 and '73

30,000 in 1871

20,000 in 1870

So what land
did you bring with you?
The little bit of dirt
between your toes
and the little bit of dirt
behind your ears?

In 1869, 15,000 buffalo
robes (most from South and
Central Alberta) shipped
through Fort Benton,
Montana.

++
the Indian Act is Canada's scar

....er...

"Kill every buffalo
you can... every
buffalo dead is an
Indian gone."

Spence is spending her days on Victoria Island in her Tipi.
Where does she spend the nights?
Burger King
Wolfing down Angus burgers
Masterful smackdown
Change the locks on her teepee.
Is it true she goes to a hotel to shower and "snack"?

ummmm

i just love those creamy hotel puff pastries

ummmmmm
Good one!! LMFAO
Look for the hotel room mini-bar
to get a thorough cleaning as well.
Wot, my hunger is not as important as an Indian's?
Raaaaaaacists!!
"Theresa Spence" is "aboriginal"?
Well then I am a Chinese man.
being 100% aboriginal shouldn't qualify you for anything
besides a free pass to beat your wife
and drink heavily
Ha Ha
She's already lost 30 pounds.
Only 3 more chins to go!
AT LAST COUNT THERE WERE 2 & ½,
This cow makes me sick.
Chief Lard butt

"I want to get rid of the Indian problem," said Duncan Campbell Scott, Deputy Superintendent of the Department of Indian Affairs, to the House of Commons in what? 1921? 1922?

History speeches

[Insert here: excerpt from the well-received "Plan For Liquidating Canada's Indian Problem Within 25 Years" presented by Dr. Diamond Jenness, Chief of Anthropology at the National Museums of Canada, to the Special Joint Committee of the Senate and the House of Commons on the *Indian Act* in 1947.]

"We have the *Oxford Book of Poetry* always handy…when I paddle Duncan reads,"
wrote Pelham Edgar, secretary to the Treaty 9 expedition, from the Abitibi in 1906.

Was it me, my father or my mother who said, as we drove through Hobbema—the location of the Montana, Samson, Ermineskin, and Louis Bull reserves—on our way to Edmonton, "What kind of people are they?"

Indian Act: "a protest may not be made under this section"

It was a silence I could not speak until I had mastered the language of silence and all the stories of silence over which I was given charge to keep.

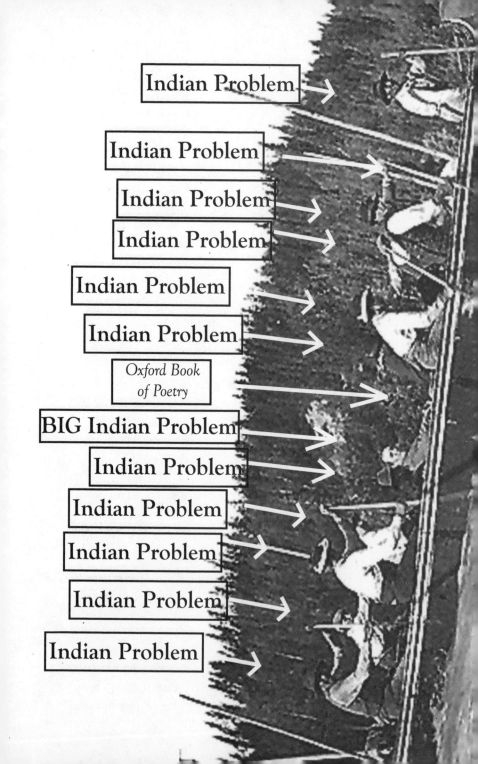

Porkyhonas!
More chins than a Chinese phone book.
Zero sympathy.
Totally!
Take a look at her.
Can you say snnniiiccckkkers!
Look in a mirror
and say Loser
Really?
we're all disgusting colonists, right?
What a load of crap.
Chief Fatty Three Chins is right on the firing line.
Hopefully she will starve herself,
I used to give the Indians the benefit of a doubt.
A bit of slack.
Not now!
Im a victim! Waaaaaa!
Someone call a WAHmbulance!
A great way to set the tone for a constructive discussion
Keep banging your little drum
impotent little man,
…quel doofus!
scum
Bravo.
Well written.
nailed it
I guess I would support Exxon Mobile
if it goes on a hunger strike.
Really clever post?
A profoundly articulated argument.
They should throw her out
send her packing
hold a semantic revolver to her head
with empty chambers
and scream

"IRISH BORN NUN
TRAINS INDIAN SCHOOL'S
DANCERS"

WWWAAAA!!!

They refused to print my comments!

the system has destroyed them

he don't pay taxes;
he don't work;
he don't do nothing
It's time to clean up the mess.
enlighten yourself o'lazy-one
Many of us live off reservation,
and maintain steady jobs, ya jac....
ubertroll
people are behind her
including loads of non-native Canadians
a few too many rain dances, drum sessions,
and tokes on the Indian peace pipe
haha!
Chief Moneybags
gimme gimme gimme
I WANT!!!! I WANT!!! I WANT!!!!!
Don't be afraid of punctuation.
gimme gimme gimme
Shut the hell up already.
Gimme More!
whining wanna be "revolutionaries"
Take the meds
step away from the computer.
Glad you caught that, saved me
from having to write the exact same thing.

[Insert here: picture of
The Kamloops Indian
Residential School
All Girls Scottish
Pipe Band, marching
in full regalia in the
Kamloops Indian
Days parade, 1962]

600 comments about a topic nobody cares about!!

What a pantload.

Remember Gustafsen Lake?

This sounds like a terrorist threat.

boo hoo, open the door to the future

M y solution was to fill a sack with doorknobs…;)

this forum is filled with doorknobs…

Give it up.

Hey, you started the 'doorknob' thingy,

not me!

I blame your people for oppressing my doorknobs

Hahaha!

And what door would you be attached to?

A well handled doorknob

attached to that door

being opened and closed,

not leading anywhere

WE ARE RESPONSIBLE
FOR THIS CALAMITOUS BREAKDOWN

and we have no idea
how to put the pieces
back together.

what we have here are
BROKEN PEOPLE

no coherent message
broken systems

Once a week, my grade school teacher would tell us a story where ten little Indian children would go out to play (she would make barefoot sounds like children running by clapping her thighs). One by one, each Indian child would hide and disappear into the forest, each with its own story. The game would go on until all of the Indian children had vanished, then we could begin our work.

115

Maybe.....just maybe
this is what it's all about!

so what now?
play the victim card,
race card,
residential school card
and the treaty rights card.
Their deck is endless.
"sacred" fill in the blank _____
hunting, burial, fishing, trapping, passage, you name it.
Bingo
the funny thing is the Indians believe
they are the ones entitled to be angry,
Note to all Natives in Canada:
trickle down economics
Those that have it keep it,
end of trickle.
spot on
It belongs to them...let's give it back
You pathetic ignorant person
I was born in Canada
I own my own land
What exactly do you imagine I give back?
22 comments and still no accusations of racism!
Time to declare "native rights"
a failed social experiment.
#getoveritnatives

WHIT PEOPLE WHO INVADED OUR LAND
PLEASE GET OFF OUR LAND
ALL OF YOUR LEASES ARE UP
Aboriginal claims are poppycock!

*Estimated death rate
in the Old Sun Indian
Residential School on the
Blackfoot reserve maybe
200 miles "as the crow
flies" from where I went to
school: 47%.*

116

The idea that we "stole" land is ridiculous.
A more advanced culture invaded and conquered.
We were never "conquered"
Get real.
After the continuing shame of being male
and white and well off,
I am almost afraid to say anything.
It makes my blood boil
blood boil   *or Lucretius*
blood boil!

WE ARE CANADIAN
AND HAVE HAD ENOUGH !!!
Well, qu'elle surprise!
One of the dippiest of the Dippers

no sappho by the smokestack

A native student once told me
her facther always felt a pain in his tonge
whenever he spoke Mohawk,
but he didn't know why.
His friend explained that whenever he spoke Mohawk
in residential school
a nun woulld put a pin in his tongue.

ι

Ooooooooooooooohhhhhhhhhhhhhhhhhhhhh!!!

What exactly are you trying to communicate?

Byaaaa!

no homer in the runoff

Peace will never come to these lands

Their culture should be treasured and preserved.
What Culture?
jogging in a circle
wearing feathers
having someone banging on a tom tom,
Hahaha ….
WAKE UP!
the chemical analysis contained no virgil
Colonial filth.
You have finally earned all the respect
of the angry, negative, old white people of Canada
Gag me with sadness.
My Wendat status Indian wife
and most other bright, self-sustaining and successful natives
mock you.
Even the Windigo
will have nothing to do with you.
Sorry honey
As a CANADIAN of Metis and Ojibway ancestry,
I am proud of my heritage
Ooh more race based distinctions.
How progressive.
If Canada survives long enough,
we'll all be Metis.
Then what?
More deadbeats
I am not a non-racist
The Irish!!
What about the Irish??
when are we all just going to be Canadians?
The white man has replaced the buffalo.

"I thought I left all this entightlement nonsense at home."
he muttered.
if I dug deep enough in my past,
I could probably find some Injun
Cool it, people.
Besides, half of you are probably white fatsoes
I have only been on a couple of reserves,
but they were awful.
garbage bags and diapers hanging in the trees
dogs left to roam,
kids with no shoes walking on the road,
dead vehicles scattered all over
alcohol bottles in the ditch.
Don't forget the Indian gangs?
So true.
they just don't care
Pathetic!
Wow you sure have a hate on for us.
Not hate
Pity

Hibernia / 73 tonnes (2011)
waterborne benzene

The cowboys won the war!
Why do I feel like we lost?

We did not loose, we won,

Bombardier / 7,752 tonnes (2011)
airborne toluene

we will cripple the very soil
u stand on

Zzzzzzzzzzz

Looks like money talks, eh.
Does it speak to any of you baboons
There's a rock ——> Go crawl under it
webpage upon webpage
of questionable sanity.
What a fuc#king joke you cretins are.
Meooow meooow,
scratch scratch.

airborne cyanide
Lakeshore Gold Corp.] 3,700 Kg (2011)

I was eleven years old
when I was first called an Indian whore!!
there was nothing we could do except cry!!!
**Ah, yes, the stuff of traditional stories,
handed down for many moons:
(Cue in the drums, chants, dances)
"Hey...nah, nah, nah, nah, nah, nah, Hey..."
"Trickster Crow took my documents."
"Bear ate my homework."
"Hey...nah, nah, nah..."**
Feather wavers, skin bangers
Hey! My posts are disappearing.
down the memory hole!!
Hoka hey!
today was a great day of Unity
with songs and dance !!!!
I've seen only smiles
and the sounds of the drum
at the round dances.

*Said Matthew Hunter of
Reverend John McDougall, hired
by the government to translate for
the Stoney (though he spoke little
Blackfoot) during Treaty 7: "He
told us to close our eyes and pray,
but when we opened them our
land was gone."*

HIY HIY!

if a Kickapoo marries a Chickasaw,
then their kids are either
Chickapoo or Kickasaw.
And if one marries a Mexican,
then the kid is a Kickacan.

Can we get a whoop whoop!?

Good god..give us a break..
Poet No More..PLEASE

Baahhh

I gotta stop reading this stuff.

The white man used to be the most feared
and ruthless race in the world.
Now look at us
Sorry, Sorry, Sorry, it's all my fault,
punish me more .
Sorry, this really bothers me but
like most Canadians,
I don't know what to do

*the Siksika, Stoney and
Tsuu T'inna on the
banks of the Red Deer.
No mention that the
Cree called the Red Deer
wâwâskêsiw-sîpiy. No
mention of the remains of
the Tail Creek des Métis
settlement a few miles
away. No mention that
we lived on land not got
by war. No mention of
the treaties we wrote and
signed with ourselves.
These things have no
plaques, no stories, only a
few mislabelled arrowheads
in a shitty museum.*

History bleaches

AS LONG AS THE SUN SHALL SHINE, AND AS LONG AS THE WATER SHALL FLOW

...EH?

Tear up the treaties!

Get out the rubber bullets and water cannons!!!!!!

use real bullets

They are a disease that needs to be gotten rid of.

Its time to cull their herd.

napalm?

u like too much video game

Lol of course

I am kidding it is sarcasm lol

jeeze people!!!!

No one sees the joke here?

lol i did not actually mean it lol

Turns out I was arguing with myself.

m^ron

It sounds like they want more than just cultural genocide.

Call in the Army.

Arrest them all

It's snowing, let's call the army.

There's a round dance, let's call the army.

What more do the Indians want, blood?

If so, give it to them!!!!!!!

simply put them down.

like a bunch of coons

And to think, people are complaining about the natives, sheesh.

Pointy white hats, anyone?

Seems like the uniform of the day.

Klanada

In the village where I was raised, a commemorative plaque was hung in 2007 to the founder of the village (Mr. Todd up) from Michigan in 1900. No mention made of Natos-Api (recorded as "Matose-Apiw" in Treaty 7) born not far from there in 1819, fabled leader of the Blackfoot Confederacy or his wife, Calf Old Woman, one of the few female Blackfoot warriors. No mention that we lived near the intersection of the lands of

jingoistic automaton

Sweet stereotyping babe

It's so like someone like you to say something like that.

That made me spurt coffee out of my nose!!

Time for you to get off your collective (_i_)'s

Why do Canadians who aren't white have to pay taxes?

Ask yourself that.

What did they do to your ancestors?

Ask yourself that.

Why do you keep repeating yourself?

Ask yourself that.

1867: 200 (exactly)

in Starbucks, I overheard some guy saying

he has ammo ready if those "indians" came by

Where do I get a head dress hunting license?

Wouldn't mind putting one of those on my wall!

!@#$%^&*'s

put away the phony Walmart beads and feathers,

stow the dime-store pipes

Our ancestors should have stamped them out long ago

now they are coming to kill and mame everyone!

an Indian War like you never seen

Careful with the threats FN.

Bwa ha ha ha ha ha ha ha ha ha.

No, seriously.

Ha ha ha ha ha ha ha.

Time to circle the wagons........

eeee..haw!!!

Listen to some of these indians.

your hatefulness

your ignorance

Your poor use of grammar

WHITES HAVE RACIALISM AGAINST THEM!!!!!!

wipe them off the face of the Earth

Fizzle In The Drizzle

Boy..it just keeps on getting better!
This is NOT going to end well..............

History teaches

Zingggggggggggggggggg.

Canada you're a strange nonsensical dream

Is this still a thing?

pre-contact: 30 million (approximately)

Is this thing still going on?

North American bison population:

Chief Spence ending her hunger strike?
Better alert KFC!
Don't forget Edmonton Tent & Awning—
she might need a new wardrobe after gorging!
Watching this come to conclusion
is like watching a train wreck about to happen.
Good grief, talk about pathetic and meaningless.
The whole thing has certainly been a farce from the get-go.
Its a tear down. Total tear down.
achieving absolutely nothing
The whole national has been awoken.....................

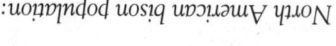

Put me to sleep.
Such bad writing.
Meaningless theatre
THE CIRCUS SHOW IS OVER.

"You will Do well to try to Innoculate the Indians by means of Blanketts, as well as to try every other method that can move to Extirpate this Erascable Race. I should be very glad your Scheme for Hunting them Down by Dogs could take Effect…" wrote Lord Jeffrey Amherst, British Commander in Chief, to Colonel Henry Bouquet during the Pontiac Rebellion of the Odawa.

Weaving new words for an old world, I originally wove this on Amherst Island, where I own land overlooking Lake Ontario, a Lafarge cement factory, a forest of wind turbines, and an Ontario Power Generation plant on the mainland. A strange congruence for a quotation many would forget. My intention was to make a tidy weave, something my grandmother could have understood, something you could see coming from Oxfordshire. But it didn't work, the writing barely decipherable, the weave too tidy for such words. This is the image, on a white blanket woven from Amherst Island wool, of that failure.

Off you go now.
Git.
Go.
Pulleeze !
no, no!
Keep going!
why stop now
the circus continues
I wonder if they will roll her out of the teepee in a wheelchair.
Let's hope they keep rolling into the sunset....
with the theme to "Rawhide"!
Or maybe the Beatles, "I'm a Loser."
... ha ha hee hee ho ho
Naw, they'll need a 4 ton forklift for sure!

Oh my God!!!!
I can't take it anymore!!!!

When you have no substance
you grasp anything you can.
I couldn't make this up!
I hope some day you feel ashamed of the things you've said.
Stop preaching at us
Quid pro quo.
Tit-for-tit.
Ughhh this is really starting to get annoying.
What a joke
Indian concerns will melt away
like a popsicle on Canada Day
Stand strong. Be proud. Don't give up!
this may be another step towards "healing"
We are better than this!
Really??
can something be divided that was never...
united in the first place........?

White Noise is composed of material harvested from 15,283 public comments posted in response to fifty-five online news articles from the *Globe and Mail*, the *National Post*, the Canadian Broadcasting Corporation, Aboriginal Peoples Television Network, *Sun News*, the *Ottawa Citizen*, the *Province*, and the *Calgary Herald* over a forty day period between December 20, 2012 and January 28, 2013. All news articles were in relation to the Idle No More protest movement and the beginning and end of the hunger strike of Theresa Spence, Chief of the Attawapiskat First Nations reserve. Idle No More started in Saskatchewan in November 2012 as a grassroots movement led by First Nations to protest recent attacks on Indigenous sovereignty, treaty rights, human rights and environmental protections by the Government of Canada. Adding to this protest, Chief Theresa Spence began her hunger strike—subsisting on a liquid diet of medicinal teas and fish broth—on December 11, 2012 demanding, among other things, a meeting between Canada's First Nations leadership, Prime Minister Stephen Harper, and the Governor General of Canada to discuss Canada's treaty relationship with First Nations. Her hunger strike ended on January 24, 2013.